How to Fall in Love in San Diego

Kevin Dublin

Copyright © 2017, 2020, 2024 Kevin Dublin

ISBN 978-1-93-584723-6 Third Edition

All rights reserved. No part of this publication may be reproduced, or stored in a retrieval system, or transmitted in any form or by any means, electronic, mechanical, photocopying, recording, or otherwise without written permission.

First edition available in print from Finishing Line Press

Publisher: Leah Maines

Editor: Christen Kincaid

The first edition of this chapbook and more are available in print via:

http://www.finishinglinepress.com
http://www.amazon.com
http://www.barnesandnoble.com

This third edition edition is available wherever books are sold.

Cover Art: David D'Amico, Chad McDonald, Glenn Beltz, Nan Palmero, Joe Wolf, Nathan Rupert

Third Edition
Book Design by Kevin Dublin

for the Kumeyaay land which nourished us

Acknowledgments

Grateful acknowledgments are offered to the wonderful editors of the following publications in which these pieces first appeared, some with different titles and/or n previous forms:

Cahaba River Literary Journal: "On Sight"

Glint Literary Journal: "Coming of Age in a Failed Platonic Love Story" "Not Kissing You"

Leipzig Glocal: "How Can You Remain in Love in San Diego" "Inflection"

Poetry Quarterly: "Finding Love in Pacific Beach with a Lover from Santee"

Quatrain.Fish: "Black Masculinity"
"Last Night You Said You Were Leaving"

Rogue Agent: "His Kind"

SOFTBLOW: "How to Fall in Love in San Francisco"
"Find the Source"
"Four Letters Dependent on Circumstance & Time"

Sunshine/Noir II: "How to Fall in Love in San Diego (1)"

Moving Poems Magazine: "Not Kissing You"

Poetry Film Live: "How Can You Remain in Love in San Diego?"

Table of Contents

Tinder Profile	3
How to Fall in Love in San Diego	4
Test Pit	6
Not Kissing You	7
How to Fall in Love in San Diego	8
When a Friend Leaves San Diego Because of Love	9
Coming of Age in a Failed Platonic Love Story	10
Find the Source	12
On Sight	13
What We Talk About When We Talk About Love in San Diego	14
Dating You Would be a Full-Time Job …	15
Four Letters Dependent on Circumstance & Time	16
The Prestige	18
Weekend	19
Last Night You Said You Were Leaving	22
His Kind	23
Each Morning	24
Finding Love in Pacific Beach with a Lover from Santee	25
Black Masculinity	26
How Can You Remain in Love in San Diego?	27
Ecstatic in Tijuana	28
Leaving San Diego	37
the magician meets the queen of cups	38
Before Work in San Francisco	40
I Should Doubt Taking an Uber to the BART Station	41
From My Personal Catalog of Your Smiles	43
Aubade	45
How to Fall in Love in San Francisco	46

Additional Acknowledgements	49
Video Poems	53
About the Author	55

I.

Tinder Profile

I am not a good lover; although, I suggest it
in every love poem is the absence
of a black man face down on pavement:
pimple on his left cheek grazed to hot pink.

How to Fall in Love in San Diego

Eat blackberry brie bites
between two fingers
at a crashed Hilton party
between the harbor
and Convention Center.
Dance to an all-white-
Otis-Redding cover band
in Hawaiian shirts.
Foot it to the dueling piano bar
only after Security checks lanyards.
Give the bartender a large tip
and advice that changes her life.
Flirt with a Swedish accent.
Pretend you're here
for a wedding
      —unless you're here
for a wedding
      —then pretend you're here
post-divorce.
Whisper in a cute brunette's ear
that her girlfriend is gorgeous,
but hug the doorman.
Learn his name
the way Goldilocks
tastes porridge—gingerly.
Tap three strangers and
ask for the restroom
in a foreign tongue
from perdon,
dónde está el baño?
to *have you seen the loo?*
Be a noble experiment.
Tell all hostesses Liam sent you.
Ask why they don't know him.
Text any number in your phone
and change the name to Liam.

Get addresses of the cutest women
and never visit them.
Snag the Uber app.
Ask where the drivers'
pink moustache is.
Tell them you heard
Hillcrest was fun, but
you'd rather drive
to an apartment—
any apartment they have keys to.
Stir gasps in distant rooms,
through every land, on each tongue
Heed cabbie's command:
Make me forget
we swoon in a desert.

Test Pit

My kitchen is messier
than when the Giza pyramids were built.
Whole apartment blown through
like a modern archaeological dig site:
duster, pointer trowels, trousers
all exposed with sheets cradling draft
from door opening.
I didn't wanna bring you home,
but you embarrass easier
and I favor the space between
a Doberman's ears
on alert like first brownie finally picked
from the sheet pan.
I try to clean: tidy the bed, move
bowls to sink,
but your purple jeans become a mosh
pit of nerds hugging
the walls of your bent ankles.

The inverted version of your body
before rear entry,
your body after: belly to bedsheets,
head high as light fixture,
bottom so pale and round and implausible—
like the slit
of our mouths, the space
where *love me*
begs to scratch way from the gullet.

NOT KISSING YOU

As inconvenient as being
the mother of breeze—
How she must name
each breeze and remember it.

Which one stirs empty chip wrapper
saddling the curb near your sandal?
I rub my cheek to be less conscious of air
untidying the hair on my forearms.

But the slight stutter of your smile—
Glow of November dusk across brow
while trolley brakes against rails in the distance.
Your lips: a strawberry perfectly split open.

How to Fall in Love in San Diego

A couple cuddles tongues on the corner of 5th and Market
Their meeting shades sunrays that heat the rain puddle
A man waits to wash his hands in

When a Friend Leaves San Diego Because of Love

My brother once wrote: *nothing is sharp or simple*—
not even the scissors used to open Amazon
boxes, not even a bite on the lower lobe
from a new lover or a sniff of the stained
front seat of a thong, not even the grey cat
with chips missing from pricked ears
who squeezes between the cement stoop
and has never climbed past the second step.

We've all been hurt like the fall of coyote's
howl after a kill in Hillcrest canyon brush.
Some of us still wear pain like a smock:
over our whole fronts and heavy at the neck.
A dead grandfather's forehead under lips,
a rough touch in Saturday showers,
or capybara's smear unscrapeable from curb.
I'll hang yours if you ask me before
you clock out. Each night with herbs
extinguishes the embers of despair a bit longer,
turns them over, buries them in sand.

There comes a time when things are sharp
and simple like splinters along the boardwalk
into bare feet, like barnacles—all sessile
and heartless glued to pier posts, like the
fenced shoreline's cut into ocean whispering
una via to the beaches. Now, you're leaving.
The one way border became too much to bear.
Your self-deportation: decolonization of the heart.

COMING OF AGE IN A FAILED PLATONIC LOVE STORY

I remember us having so much fun you took a dump
behind an oak tree because you didn't wanna walk home.
It was fall, and you described the leaves' cold scratch
as if it were trying to pick thick pudding from a tight space,
spoon brittling away between fingertips from the weight.

For several days we'd watch the white ritual of it harden.
Let scavengers pick at it like cruel punishment for knowing
we put it there. Six months after, you invited me to my first
cypher. An impromptu group of hoodies and windbreakers
leaning against gymnasium walls like living graffiti.

One guy—Green Eyes was left behind so many times
he was twice the size of the next cat, had a mustache—
not peach fuzz, but the real kind you couldn't cut
with bare clippers. He was the type'a light skin
you would call m'zungu because it was so probable.

And his bars reflected 'em too, *Like Bishop from Juice—*
you don't know the ledge, so why I'm messin' witchu? /
Crazy dark skin cat who think he can rap? /
Here's five bullets for you / BLAP BLAP BLAP BLAP BLAP /
Take that, ay son, pass me his shoes! /

And the crowd ouuuu'd like they heard "Hit em Up"
for the first time. And he walked the line, stomping
the aluminum of each lyricist's pride. It got to the point
that nobody had anything to offer him, so he twisted
his snap cap back forward and we all wafted in its silence.

'Til my cousin spit lines at me: Stuff about how I'd pee the bed,
piss bucket next to mattress, so I'd never miss. Most of it
wasn't true. I was about to not be ten, knew what he was doing.
High school cliquelessness was not cool and these guys were—
Green Eyes' irises widening with each bar stymied in front of me.

And I knew I should take it. These cats didn't even know
my name and I could only rap along to tapes, had no rep,
and went to a different school. Plus they had never seen me
nearly naked or palmed a conversation that changed my life:
You wanna end up like the brothas at Peabody's house, fool?

That was it, but still. I kept *crack kills* closer than the cereal bowl
on Saturday morning during Dragonball Z. Usually next to you,
and here you were transitioning from youth—Static glider high.
Shocking. And when you said the line about my dead mama,
I wanted to cry—throat-stomp you against pavement and cry.

I wanted to say we'd grow up and always be in touch.
If there was an entire country between us, it'd mean nothing.
Your opinion: like glitter, impossible to get rid of, except useful.
This wasn't the last Saturday.
I'd embrace you first after each child was born—miss you
the way clouds miss rain and plead to sun *evaporate*.

I'd eulogize you when you died. Break a pact. Tell a congregation
about the time you dropped a deuce behind an oak tree—
the first acknowledgement of it ever between my lips.
Instead, I mentioned it in a terrible freestyle that barely rhymed
to nine dudes who were nothing to me but everything to you.

Find the Source

Stop.

Run backwards through the door you've entered,
cross the intersection, then glance both ways.
The crosswalk sign will switch to orange hand.

Reach into your khaki pocket
where a cell phone will leap into your grasp.
Let your clammy palm press it to your face then state,
og ut vuh ye ee-ross.

Gape at the short brunette woman in burgundy
stepping rearfirst from the Golden Hill café;
notice she's alluring, then notice her tears,
then last see her figure as a burly jerk barks,
oo-e-khuf, before she jostles into him and
disappears around a corner.

Play.

On Sight

Your glance: an invitation tied with red ribbon.
An introduction like jazz trumpet solo by Lee Morgan:
smooth and scarred, the skin of the knee, mushrooms
on tongue. Our attraction: a sniper's finger testing
trigger. Kisses: a pull without release. Our sex:
kickback cradled into shoulder. The aim: to make
me fall. All I remember is falling. I'm still trembling—
will always tremble 'til I'm nothing but dust, sunlit—
orphaned as bits of torn skin flaking wind. The rest
just residue washed from crevices of your open palms.
Next morning: heavy yet squishy like sans serif waiting—
a warning: attraction can transcend most sanity.

What We Talk About When We Talk About Love in San Diego

nestled in a garage complex, etched into valley
which smells like gasoline and rain falling,
notice our breath mossing its way onto window,
startled at headlights leaving us one car from empty
like a head two seconds from sleeping on
the chilled side of pillowcases: there's a TARDIS;
black hair cut short under skullcap; infinite number
of socks for centipedes; what might be dipped in beer
with cinnamon on top: expensive waffles, falafel,
collapsed soufflé before a specially made kahlua, amaretto,
Boston cream-pie cake shot; hatred of needles; the taste
of mayonnaise; the glory of peanut butter on popcorn—

The car parked, five seconds from stalling conversation.
Here, a lock unlocks in our left eyes: time sutures so neatly
we forget how we were wounded and wake to the plump,
sharp-eyed butterfly of desire—the only pollinator
in the desert of flourishing, windshield wiperless,
but specked with drizzle and whispers of what's
forgotten. That is San Diego. San Diego, beautiful
like a lick of foreign tongue. We reckon. Oh, we reckon.

More has been lost than what people have ever found
in foreign places. One day we'll all be foreign. Even fireflies
will lose the light in their bodies and be alone. But,
if we've learned anything from closed strip malls
covering dismissed graves at least a league deep,
it's that nothing, not the voluminous layers of earth,
not the crunch of steps, not the constant rush of freeway,
not even the art of all disorganized noise that is living
can silence the quiet ringing of the dead's memory of touch.

Dating You Would be a Full-Time Job with Little Security and Sub-Standard Benefits

Yet sometimes we end up in situations that involve genitals:
usually lasting the quiet, blue hour before dew catches light.

You chatter cheeky promises post-coitus to piss me off,
Like: *you'll always come first*, to keep me awake—so I admire

your back: smooth like taupe face of a child
dozing with an open mouth against windowpane.

You sleep-rhyme words that don't rhyme.
Voice twists *come in* to sound like *trust me*.

Infatuation lets you believe there's just waiting, like the dark
of sleep, what we need just happens—only heavier.

Dreams teach carousels are the best place for orgasms:
with zebra smiles full of teeth, lit by glow worm moon.

Four Letters Dependent on Circumstance & Time

How many poets have praised the moon?
Still, moon has no moonlit lover:

glow empties each morning alone:
no moonlit fool to moon.

Who will solve this problem?
The one with touch fickle like a yawn:

she's blue when I hear her voice
singing borrowed song:

I'm So Tired of Being Alone
inside this woman's mouth

over orange bitters and vermouth,
we splay meeting words:

You say you experiment,
but you're no scientist,

so I ask what
you're doing through the week—

Who moves to Australia for a boy?
There's men here who massage so excellent

they get yelled at for making breath
all inhales with three letters and a glance

tied like slipknot. A man who will remember
your name as two fingers split, slid from left cheek to chin.

Men who can write moonlit poems upside down
over spirits—including "g" and "s" despite

the difficulty of all words turned over:
drunk, like the call of lone nightjar,

he'll slip home through cracked door
forgotten as fingertip on light switch.

THE PRESTIGE

These days every love poem has lovers.
This makes them similar to old love poems.
Love is pasted together kisses which become
a papier-mâché Eiffel Tower with I Love You
cursived at the base. Usually in red ink
beside a pressed mauve scribble off the page,
to broken chalk and five clenched fingers
yearning to moan. So much sex in love poems,
of course, there's carnal embrace and shadow,
but what about the thick stickiness left
in the end? Let's talk about it. Do more than skirt
or shoulder it. Hear your mint green chortle
after the most inappropriate joke. The rise
of your eyebrows at its initial mention—
heartbeat and fingertip perspiration.
My open palm waves above table
like it was a love poem, and when you blush, it
matches the shade of your lips, color of gull flight—
fussy pink above butterfly orange sunset. Shit
you only read in a love poem these days: longing
evaporating from page like black pavement
emitting heat haze: *wait* pinched from paper
at the *W* and rubbed between fingers 'til
it's only *T*. Still, it's just a magic trick with letters.
An acknowledgement of artifice with craft
as the pledge—the turn in my stomach when
you feel my hand on your chin, and—alakazam: *kiss*.

Weekend

It's only Sunday another seven minutes,
and Monday means goodbye.
The moon jealous just enough as we lie
on our backs while scratching words to keep stars
in view. You pucker when you write p's.
Sometimes, I alliterate only for possibility
or reminder of your kiss. Your profiled silhouette
lit at the edges by streetlamps, another phantom
of our pleasant fiction. It's only Sunday…

And Monday means goodbye.

Headlights casually scalp midnight darkness
the way any great warrior does: indiscriminately,
all at once. But that's an ending.
And all of your endings betray your beginnings.
The truth obscured for so long along country
roads: behind briar brush, between muddy
bootprints hardened at the sole of red oak roots.
How many changes of shoes—how many
soaked up tank tops—how many messy
buns and teeth-heavy smiles does it take
to drive across ten states with a toxic darling
who will undo you? You unravel him
like loose thread of ballet slipper, with vengeance.
No, vengeance isn't the correct word: love is.
I want to tell you, but it's Sunday…

And Monday means goodbye.

Hello—who is this? /
Sippin' finished dregs with–
caramel macchiato scented chin/
head tilted like so in italics—
hidden left curve of the nose/
the only bit exposed beneath sunglassed—

and Starbucks-cupped face/

This is how I met you.

Trumpet kicks a head back
on stage, feet come to blows
with the dance floor—you join in—
we jump that bitch to heavy
percussion 'til we entangle.

No, this is how I met you.

With poetry and lips,
the same rules apply:
be soft—do hard things.

It's hardest when it's on Sunday…
And Monday means goodbye.

Goodbye reminds me
to *mean what you put your mouth on*
whether it's words or the silent parts of a body.
I just want to win the lottery—
go on Tinder dates for the rest of my life.
One point three billion bits of moonlight sipped
from chipped whiskey glasses with poorly-washed fog
at the bottom. How many more boys would blush,
harden, domino from your push through South Park,
Grantville, Ocean Beach? You'd still desire everything:
curbside rolling chairs ridden down hilltop streets at three a.m.,
refusing to yield at stop signs, especially on Mondays—
and in protest—when no one else believed in hip-hop
after the thrift shops closed. My dear walking hyperbole,
it's the last minute of Sunday. *And Monday means goodbye.*
Means *migration*: an animal form of leaving.

You'll ask me not to shorten or shrink this infinity—
mostly because it makes you sound like a slut,

which you aren't. You're a business partner after last call,
a scholar of feminism after two hits of indica,
a wearer of bum hats traded for burritos
who hates racist animals under four feet long.
You know, most people fear caring, no matter the return.
They're afraid of skin splitting at the chest and another
whole person tearing out. But we know better.
There will be a day when we praise stitches.

It's Monday. It's Monday. It's Monday. It's Monday.

Last Night You Said You Were Leaving

This morning:
your voice, the house sparrow's
step on dried ash leaves.

His Kind

after Anne Sexton, Sylvia Plath & Edna St. Vincent Millay

I have stumbled home rigid, warming
her shoulders like black coat. I had called her,
coaxed her with conversation,
dinner, a movie and salsa night.
I wore a scent. I wore slacks. I wore a shirt
which fit and hid the fat usurping my belly.
Conveyed the cabernet on my lips
after picking up the tab.
I have known his kind.

I have pulled out and played my part,
groaned, let her take life onto her heart,
grinning a blonde twitch. I have been
where I could not fit. I felt ridges
as she stretched imagination to fathom
father's response. I did not make her say *daddy*.
I did not. I did suggest she get comfortable
after she came in and asked for nightcap.
I have been his kind.

I have woken to empty bed
by birdsong—chit chit twee, chit chit twee—
by gleam of dawn's chorus against window.
I have hailed to bathroom, asking,
would you like breakfast? Heard nothing, knew
she used the moon to hex into my home.
I know what I know:
Men like me aren't men, quite.
I am his kind.

Each Morning

my skin is so dark
it makes night against your body—
my body, your first evening

Finding Love in Pacific Beach with a Lover from Santee

I imagine my father young, swaying, and castrated
just for having half of what we're doing in his head.
It's enough to make you redden—make me rigid.

You once told me my teeth and the blinks of eyes
were the only things distinct from darkness.
Now I exist naked, pressed on your pale canvas.

Somewhere past your window, under high beams,
leans another young woman so unloved she lies
down for phallus after phallus after phallus.

Years from now you'll marry a white truck driver
who'll give you two children, to whom he'll give
drunken bruises you'll excuse because you believe

what he bawls is true; *he is the best
an ex-nigger-lover like you can do.*

BLACK MASCULINITY

O holy metamorphosis of surrender!
Slow as ocean's collection, drop by drop,
to become ocean. All you have to do is cry.

How Can You Remain in Love in San Diego?

Today, the screen froze when *End Call* was pressed.
No feedback, just the illick between fingertip and glass.
We always said goodbye too soon: before a question,
before a *right quick*, before *I love you*. Today,
like chill of shadow stroking cheek, was only goodbye.

I sat—right in the grass. Where the hours pulled
themselves onto my lap and asked to be cradled.
Silent as the oval of my mouth when you said
you wanted to be pregnant at a car dealership
during an argument about curly fries & condiments.

What will become of our children? They will suffer
the rough edge of tenderness from another father,
another mother. Your goodbye is an earthquake.
The rest of life aftershocks at the realization: we were
tectonic & unaware with no promise of tremors' stop.

I am afraid you will remember me as a wooden ladder
or even worse, forget I was. And I'll remember you
as a disaster. Unable to recall how you swallowed yawns
like milk, the attractiveness of how slow you'd waddle—
so slow I'd miss your step—dust collected on magenta toes.

When we met, we were incredibly far from the desert.
I thought you were too good for me. I didn't think
you'd speak. You said *there's a delay* in my handsomeness.
The *ness* unsteadily climbed from your tongue to lips.
I watched it fog, pillow in the air—brace a snowflake's fall.

Ecstatic in Tijuana

Tu no sabes qué sé
¿Qué es saber? tocar el árbol
El árbol es vida del niños
Niñez es saber y saber es
El Río dejando y nunca dejando

Donde estas?

Leaning over the Coko Bongo railing as bottles open.
11:40 flashed on phone screen in English and Spanish for
the transexual with legs that question gender and a man
whose sex waves as inflated, arm-flailing taxi stands waves,
turns as first fold of a phone number on a small, torn sheet.

It's here. Esta aqui, no alli! Where we're destined
to be. Flowing banners stilled against the fenced
building to the snare drum's beat, ignoring the breeze.
Viento viento todo viento.

He stops your stare with a sweating face, asks your state: below
ugly immaculate curls, eyes opened wider than Brooklyn
stretched slices yet to be sliced. Mouth impossible *oh*
and words that wish to be palabras—almost still
letras holding hands. Don't forget. It will also grace
your son's visage on Sundays at the edge of a bridge's
concrete stumbling over itself onto the asphalt like left
over rice at Thai with her. Her—the reminder of most
you aren't but want to be: *fit, fit, fit, fit.*

With stomach that slouches, even tilted back in a lounge
chair—with masculine that ends in question mark,
not an exclamation point and prefers to
lend smiles to strangers. One who forgets how to scowl
even when trying to merge onto the 15 North from the 8
and a white 3 series BMW forces you to Friars East—
where it feels safe. Home can be anywhere

with the warrior pose stretch of advice and
where destiny comes smooth as the fifth Corona
in the first hour of Sunday. La primera, you believe.
You believe so deeply you can never remember
which light switch is the dim one sans fan.

De donde eres?

Hand fidgeting like you don't know where you're from,
like you're sleepwalking in the wrong house
because every dream in a house is the house
you were born ten minutes from. The one
next to the only longleaf pine left in the hood
despite it once being a forest. There's houses,
community action, and apple trees and a pear
tree which only bears fruit for blue jays
and cardinals instead. Between the apple
and pear tree are two memories: one as frivolous as
burying a Skittle and watering it for a week. Two:
one of the oldest, a 1970's console record player
gifted for a 15 year old's wedding 20 years later
and a console TV bought with bits of six paychecks
at the end of a school hall reached by a professional's
mop. Between those two: a corner window tight in
a thin, yellow dress to match the house paint, to contrast
the metal green chairs who have always wanted to rock,
but are self-conscious beneath beautiful bodies and
desperately immune to wind. This corner—
only accessible to slender forms: the toddler with blankets
and cradled, aching canines. *Shhhhhhhhh—
we're not supposed to be inside*, especially when
we have worms, especially when we cough them up
like insecurity—all brown and wriggled with living
and when the edges scratch off epidermis like a lottery
ticket that doesn't win. It was your last ten dollars
and the light bill is due. How can you add two bedrooms
and plumbing without electricity and nine mouths to feed
with another jaw testing itself in a wet jelly filled space?

That is my memory even if I was incapable of knowing.

I, the unfit of body, of masculinity, of patience
have just learned to fit dead and a question mark
in the same space of the mouth as *I love you*.
It's practice, like conjugating verbs in foreign tongue:
jugar, jugo, jugares. Fuck the irregular. Fuck it at three,
at nine, at sixteen, at twenty-five. We'll never learn
to rock in chairs not destined for it—on improper legs
attempting to stand from so much loss. It's as deep
in your son's five year old eyes as the center of Tahoe—
A lake I want to hug two bodies in front of and whisper
*it's beautiful when you're able to take a puzzle piece made to be
center of the moon and fit it with cooled desert sand*. One was
not meant to be so far from the earth that it begs waters come
closer—and the other withstands destruction so powerfully
it doesn't, it becomes something else entirely. I apologize.
I was incorrect. His eyes are several leagues deeper and swell
over on those Sundays after bacon, pancakes, or Jack
in the Box—because parents aren't perfect.
At least we brush their teeth most nights at 7:33
before bed on weekdays. At 8:30 on the weekends, but
much later on those Saturdays. We have to bag the skin
beneath the eyes for Sundays. Bag them with *Green Eggs
& Ham*, Monopoly on a tablet beneath a comforter, and
the same song hummed like a single track on a playlist forced
to repeat like eastern Carolina sharecroppers who learned
this was what white people called their freedom. Those
who would find solace and hope on faces of even the ugliest
large-nosed, tooth-peeking smiles, though weary in the hands,
weary in the legs, weary in the cotton picking soul
from the plant's alert security guard who pricks and isn't able
to be soothed by sole peanut butter sandwich on hardened
bread. I do not *wish* or *deseo* on this side of the Baja border
for this pain. *Dolor*—both incomplete words—sorrow: two
sizes too small even for just the front of connotation's foot.

This foot: cocktail-splashed and stepped on 'til balcony's edge.

Where there's a white light between the colored even here
red and blue, bright and smeared jester smile, shadowed
eyes on each Halloween face. What some see as wasted
potential, I call living—like bass line was the oxygen
of every track blasted from cars on my block. My block—
where underpass was a mouth and Market St. the esophagus.

De donde vengo yo!

Buses—weekday mornings' breakfast—Buses
weekday afternoons' vomit. Smithfield was sick.
1746 was not when she was settled. She never was.
And my grandparents saw the signs on both sides.
They were distant cousins kept by her lies for too long.
She is not a kind lover. Her hand uninvited at the necks
of men who look like me. German shepherd broken
off the chain, jealous of another's heat.

De Donde vengo yo!

My parents
left her for North. They were not afraid of work
like I am not afraid of privilege. Integrated schools—
a privilege. Entrance of library through rotating doors—
privilege—whistling in proximity of women: a problem.
My father once laughed at nineteen and the air wasn't
shielded between his teeth. He is chased to this day
with fear and mistrust clenched in his armpit.

All the way to Newark, New Jersey and back—
where tanks can roam freely on the streets:
barrel and muzzle shut out behind cheap curtains.
There are still riots, despite the roadwheel and track-tred.

De donde vengo yo!

They returned with seven children and made two more
to avoid ending their poverty. Prosperity introduced cordially
like foreigner with no lingua franca and only the hands.

Now, on some Mondays, in my suit, I take a broom and sweep
the office, contemplate, this is how my father fed our family.
Brother, no brothers, all of us.
Those born with similar placenta and you, of another
with a thinner nose made to lift glasses.
We each know this pulled apart Pangea—this tectonic shifting
of the heart. And you, whose name might've been Ghost Step
or Lost Walker in another life, know your daughter's eyes are
your mother's but keener. They will see each continent
many times over and deeply without worry—even after
we are both dust. I ask to be blessed with your fortitude,
and I don't even know what language lent English this root.
Stand, tall as you do, leaning into the smoothest balcony rail
we've leaned into. It's only, next to you, I remember
there are people beneath us on the path to heaven. We'll forget
hell is possible at the end of blankets. Saturdays
when being alone might mean the spider's legs or the snake's
belly or the scorpion's pincers against what must be the tender
body of regret. How do we have phone service to connect
with others from this side of a wall which extends to blemish
the ocean? I want to walk and swim over with you
like so many que quieren sus hijos a querer.
If we don't make it, we're not fit.

A donde vas?

Deseas algo mas
Me gusta caer ...

Are we brave enough?

Taxi libre!
Now I need you! Arm lifted like toasting escape at the far end of the table.

Taxi libre!
Is the journey long?

Taxi libre!

Will you swerve the corners like they may crumble
if not protected by the sheer speed of your tires' passing?
Taxi libre!
Si! hablo un poco español, pero entiendo mucho mas!

Taxi libre!
Please, teach me what I do not know!
Your tongue begs to be comfortable in my mouth.

Taxi libre!
I was so embarrassed when I didn't have the sack to carry
Esteban! Do you remember me?
We met two years ago in September at Poesia Caracol!

Taxi libre!
Take me from the warm brown-eyed glances
of these lovely dancing women! The wonder
around their irises of how or whether I desire them
makes me so uncomfortable I must dance alone.

Taxi libre!
How did other men acquire being a man?
Para mi—no soy hombre, yo estoy hombre—
o, soy un niño.

Taxi libre!
See, I've already exhausted my tongue and it sits
in the darkest corner of the nightclub, solo
after hours without a break on the dance floor,
gyrating with your language.

Taxi libre!
I'm only twenty-eight. How is my right knee damaged from
bragging about a layup in the face of a tall seventh grader?
See, a child, and it pains me anytime I sit too long
or wander canyon six brushes from coyote's snarl
and a homeless snore, comfortable at home.

Taxi libre!

Where did I plead you to take me?

Taxi libre.
Make space between my words and your right ear invisible:
kisses are treated like all of my bad decisions. I give too many
to the eager and save the rest for too long.
Even when I have missed calls from lips sweeter,
softer than Krispy Kreme donuts—hot signed and melting
as neon in the mouth. I do not call back. I could not bear
failing her voice's mezcal lilt, swallowed, somehow, against
my eardrum, smoky at the back of my throat.

Taxi libre.
Does this count as a taxi cab confession?
There was no sex; though, I do have stories,
but they're in quiet blonde strands crowding
the inside of my black cardigan. They are
at sticky edges of black lace thongs
which materialize in my backseat. So common-
looking splayed on my leather interior
I appreciate, but wish I could've owned a decade ago—

Taxi libre.
Forgive my first world problems. I smell the salt,
the ocean mixed with light smoke from what
must be something meaty comforted by tortilla—eating—
what we have in common, calling—a way of calming,
all these teeth into ground wheat flour. Swallowing
disco panic. Recalling in the fever, Quincy Jones' voice:
all that will be left when we are gone is water and song.
No, *the last thing to leave this planet will be water and music,*
Quiero saber todo necisito saber, so I drink water
And to the music, like trees guided by wind's hand—
qué baila—let us dance like children.

II.

Leaving San Diego

What else is as inevitable as leaving
San Diego and death?
Even when I'm so low,
I no longer believe.
These days, I seek what's above,
find time to be alone. Desire in
the heart plucked like first grey hair.
So I drive further and further,
'til something around me or
something within me dies.

THE MAGICIAN MEETS THE QUEEN OF CUPS

there is a space in my body filled with incantations—
& in them, is a hex for all world leaders who support incrementalism
and contest progress. it begins with the holiest of repetition:
resist *resist* *resist*. alongside simple lessons:
spell *sky* into a pool of water with your pointer finger, it will rain.
scratch *fire* with a thumb into dry wood, then whisper *light*
& watch flames. the same does not apply for *love* onto a lover's back
because there is a limit, even to witchcraft.   especially in abstract.

perhaps love is a dahlia grown from rainfall & sunlight,
like all wildflowers. i believed that once.   i did—was wrong. perhaps
love is the hand fitting a lit cigarette between the bleedings lips of
a stranger gritting out *they tell me to go home, but i was born here.*
or perhaps love is in the limp scuttle of one pigeon to another
pigeon, through rain, past shuffling boots & heels & sneakers, &
flats to simply rest a pumping neck onto the chest of another pigeon.

before i met you.   i've seen the body sink,
lose its soul like a latex helium balloon in old age lowering.
i've seen the sun rise in another language over foreign hillsides
and urban mesas. i've heard elected hatred spew melting
mountain glaciers worth of reminders that the united states
of america has yet to be made into what it ought to be. i've heard
curses quoted in history lectures, on daily news, in youtube videos
directed at bodies which look like mine. i've twice felt the earth open
and offer through another human, which i share resemblance.
 i've tasted the smell of rain   *drip*drop*drip*
before a hurricane which would claim half of several counties
& winds snatch hundreds of houses and trees in its hands.

it is only after all of this & reading a million lines of poetry &
crossing the two hundred thousand miles mark on a used elantra
over a decade old that i drove until the engine exploded
on a california freeway mess in the middle of the night & flying

to the most expensive american city for a job I never worked
but knew someone, so nepotism finally worked in our favor,
& skipped between the cracks of feces-speckled geary street
into a bar for a bourbon & ginger beer & saw a girl.

a girl scribbling in a little red notebook, a notebook she would lose,
& i knew i had to meet her. it is only after all of this
all of this   that i believe less in the necessity of my own magic.
& there is truly something greater than the mystical influence
of a body, believe   believe that I might have
met   you, darling, manic mistress of blonde tension.
you, merlot lipstick, beautiful remedy for the envy of street pigeons.

Before Work in San Francisco

I strolled northeast on Hyde Street
all the way to Fisherman's Wharf before morning
spoiled on concrete slabs facing the Golden Gate
Bridge. Alcatraz at my back, I sidle
behind a curator who unlocks the side
entrance of Chloe Gallery. I use their coffee
maker because I refuse Starbucks next door.
Plus, there's no feminist paintings in chain cafés,
not a one, especially not still life with Manolo Blanniks
slipped off at hot tub edge next to three thirty-
year-old bottles of wine uncorked for one night:
tops chocolate-smeared and half foiled. A Felini
DVD is lasered inside—it's reflected in the empty
glasses so close they almost tink. When I leave
the gallery, it's only because I've been discovered,
and the walk back to Market Street is an hour,
and I only have forty minutes to get there.
I'll be late because it's Thursday, and it's sunny.
I don't need a paycheck. I just need my soul saved.

I Should Doubt Taking an Uber to the BART Station

with you, because it feels lazy
because I was raised
saving McDonald's napkins
and plastic bags from Piggly Wiggly.
Because, tonight, we've just eaten
in an expensive restaurant
overlooking Canadian geese on a lake.
We know it's expensive because
chalet is in its name, because
they refuse to make grilled cheese,
because the geese aggressively duck
their heads into rough waters
as if they were being baptized mid-sneeze.

Seriously, sixty of the ninety dollar check
must've come from a fowl tax
because there's no way we had that much
to eat or drink. Maybe
it's because we were underdressed.
Maybe it's because I left a large tip
to prove I could to the brother serving us,
though, his service was less to us
than those in other seats.
But one could see a feather and keep it
as a bookmark for a Bible, not knowing
it's from an asshole of a goose.
One could step on a used condom
on Geary Street, fresh semen stuck
on the front soles of your new loafers
and not know it's from the fourth floor
window of a young couple who
share a studio and have just made love
for the first time after a year
of pointless sex.

When we leave, I'd like to walk with you,

read you love sonnets beneath a tree,
but puddle-butt looks good on no one—
it's raining in Oakland, and you tell me
it's been a long time since I've written
you a poem as saltgrass two-steps
in first fuzz of streetlamp. I open umbrella
to avoid drizzle frizzling your hair
or dampening your smile while you tap
our destination into the app.

In the car, you cuddle close:
lapped shoulder, fingers folded
into mine like loaf of marble rye—
pale entwined with the black,
eyelids quietly home at eyelid base.
I notice nothing new. Not this time.
Even as bars of shadow appear
and are banished by borrowed yellow light
from your forehead to chin. No, not really
yellow, but the color plucked sunflower petals
would bleed in the dark. Your nose is there,
then gone; and there, then gone again
in quadrilaterals of light. I might've whispered
something I wasn't ready to admit, too
embarrassed to write. Lips from alternate
future proving quantum entanglement legit.
I could write about how it changed me,
and it'd make this worthy, make it a love poem.

At our stop, I start at your thighs
to stir you—because I'm a pervert
and because—your thighs.
I can't feel lazy when I have opportunity
to cuddle you—even in sloppy lines
with poor enjambment and silly puns.
Maybe it's all because I'm free
to not doubt anything with you, except
everything else.

From My Personal Catalog of Your Smiles

The eyes closed, full-toothed, mid-kiss smile
The just noticed our noses are touching variant
with only the top row of teeth
The post-third orgasm, slackjaw joyous smile
The post-second orgasm, slurred sentence of *more*
The variant where words never arrive
The variant when you say my name before
The variant when you say my name after and
your tongue lingers on the roof
of your mouth, savoring
the final syllable.

The sassy and you know it, manic pixie smile:
like after you say *I'm not jealous.*
Bitches just need to respect who your queen is.
The smile that leaks from uncertainty:
are you laughing at me?
The early spill of laughter, overtaking kinky smile
when you realize *I'm laughing with you*, but
you just weren't laughing yet.

The slick smile between an unintended pause
and a secret beneath comforter.
Steak-tough smiles when I make self-aware, non-intersectional
comments to laugh to keep from crying
Faux smile to calm my worry, wall yourself from qualms and care,
for protection when my African spider spirit crawls too far,
carrying Bill Cosby's body, sacked, to preserve him
with a mistaken *at least*. I'm sorry for that smile,
sorry you felt you had to make it,
sorry your mother and mother's mother
and grandmother's mother and their men made you feel
you had to make it. Fuck the patriarchy and my part in it.
We don't deserve a smile.

What does deserve a smile is a black and white,

dapple-skinned great dane
on a long leash to whom you offer a smile freely, despite
the rain and heavy-grey fuzzy-dim light beneath our umbrella.
The smile when you whisper, *here's to my sweet Satan*.

The twenty-first type of smile you have is the quiet,
private smile, in bed when you turn away to spoon.
I only know it exists because I've heard your cheeks
furl outward. I hope to see it one day. The way
you smile, ecstatic, during belly rubs: half-exhales,
half-heaven. The smile after a joking *no*,
before another stomach-grumble or a fart
full of chow mein and Sunday lust.

The closest smile. The one which comes instead of a kiss,
when your chapstick is freshest, full of pumpkin spice.
The smiles while dreaming. In the half-hour of dusty light,
on fog-cold San Francisco mornings—how they seem
to speak to dawn in a tap code. *I'm not dreaming of him.
I'm not dreaming of him. I'm not.* God calls you a liar
and lets the light win. Each time.

A new smile: when I mention this list exists—casual,
doubtful above running kitchen sink.

A new smile: when I finish reading it to you.

Aubade
for Kbzz

Ever since I've wanted, I've wanted you
to hold, whisper to, keep warm in cold, scratch
on paper, drink neat Jack 'til we collapse
and gel au naturel to *soixante-dix*
repeated by needle in a deep groove.

Soixante-dix. Soixante-dix. Soixante-dix.

The silence after so much noise statics—
swabs vibrations heavy, sweaty on our tongues.
If I were to speak, I'd lose control.
But let all mortal flesh keep silent.

There is holiness we can only approach
in the hollow of bottles. We don't know it,
invoke His name from pristine carpet facing east,
thinking *to Love be the glory for the great things She has done*
as the first ohmmmms of sun peek through.

How to Fall in Love in San Francisco

Now curled in bed alone, eyelids slide open
notice the cold losing to light
on the window. A yellow house finch
peeks from shrubbery. Then another
and another lands. They flit as if
they know I've never been so happy
watching condensation chip from glass.
It is better than a North Beach night
after Golden Sardine, after a loft
party found because I was invited
by two potential lovers on the bus,
after waking up between vintage thrift shops
in the Mission clutching a white album sleeve
with the record label scratched off.
This window, gently dissolving night's work,
is precious, though, I'm tired, though, I must pee.
I won't leave this spot. I won't go back to sleep.
This morning's arrival is slower than most.
I, in blue and white and grey striped pajamas
bought from Wal-Mart in East Bay. You, hunched,
in some ugly green jacket buying them.
The green: the shade a first grader might color
ninja turtle poop: probably Michelangelo's.
It's hard to believe a moment ever existed
when I didn't love you. When I had opportunity
to admire you each morning and passed the mirror.
It's embarrassing that I was with you
so many times and wasn't with you—what a waste,
especially when I've had you to myself, especially
since miles down in a dying Mexican lake without a river
or ocean there is a mole salamander that lives
its entire life without metamorphosis. I am no kin
to axolotl. Now subtle as yawn's transfer from crust
around my mouth to frostlessness on glass. I know
I'll never need to wait for any other moment.
Not even for the latest iPhone, or gaming console, or

in any concert line: Phoenix, you begin when I arrive!
See it! The glass is clearing and clear and
being has become more real than the body,
like cloud's shift allowing a slice of dawn's light
and hits where a leaf falls from eucalyptus tree:
its weight tested by the air, hovering,
as I step from the bed, we are beautiful—
even as the world beyond ashes and burns.
May we wake each morning and remember it.

Additional Acknowledgements

The longest piece of language I could ever write would contain a thank you to everyone who deserves it. May these acknowledgements be but the smallest token toward my eternal debt to you all. Thank you to my editors at Finishing Line Press who accepted this manuscript and published it in print: to Christen Kincaid, Leah Maines, Kevin Maines, Elizabeth Maines, the editorial assistants, and all of the team who were so kind and patient and allowed me to retain electronic rights of this chapbook.

Gratitude to Sandra Alcosser, Marilyn Chin, and Ilya Kaminsky for your guidance and thoughts on these poems.

Thank you to Elizabeth Aeby, Hari Alluri, Michael Benedetto, Meghan Bliss, Erica Blunt, Ana Bosch, Garrett Bryant, Amber Carpenter-Sanford, Mallory Christianson, Karla Cordero, Jessica Cory, Luke Crane, Kaitlyn Dyer, Nicole Aubrey Edwards, Jesus Esparza, Amanda Fuller, Charlie Griggs, Austin Harold, Dani Heinemeyer, Danielle Hunt, Arthur Kayzakian, Carlos Kelly, Ryan Kelly, Breeann Kirby, Alyssabeth Knerr, Jen Lagerdrost, Amie Macbeth, Carolann Madden, Rachel Gellman Martin, Stephen Mason, Esra Uzun Mason, Makeba McLeod, Chelsie Meredith, Carly Joy Miller, Binh Nguyen, Samantha Randolph, Dave Rhei, Jonathan Rodley, Kayla Rodney, Gabriel Rubi, Ron Salisbury, Dillon Scalzo, Janel Spencer, Scott Stewart, and Omer Zalmanowitz for their eyes or their hearts or their heads and sometimes all three towards these poems and others.

Thank you to Alex Albright, John Hoppenthaler, and Andrea Kitta for your wisdom and support in becoming a better writer by writing better and better understanding writing. To Lavonne Adams, Sandra Alcosser, to Tim Bass, to Margaret Bauer, to Marilyn Chin, to Mark Cox, to Angela Dotson, to Katie Farris, to Hal Jaffe, to Ilya Kaminsky, to Ruth Mills, to Malena Mörling, to Dan Noland, to Kathy Rugoff, to Lee Tatum, to Luke Whisnant, to Michael White for the same.

To the Watering Hole and to the inspirational well water from which we first drank and continue to drink. To Kwame Dawes, to Nikky Finney, to Patricia Smith, to Frank X Walker. Thank you, Monifa Lemons. Thank you, Candace Wiley.

Thank you to the writers I admire and was lucky enough to call friends when my foundations as a writer were still being set, whose work or words I still return to and learn from. To Vivian Bahr, to Maya Beerbower, to Will Coppage, to Rachel Dickerson, to Jean Jones, to Carter Monroe, to Lee Nance, to Elizabeth Niederheiser, to Ana Ribeiro, to Fernando Sanders, to Marty Silverthorne, to Tyler David Sparks, to Daniel Nathan Terry, to Scott Urban, to Jeff Wyatt, to Andrea Young.

Thank you to my fellow writers and partners in education. To Marc Alford, to Lisa Andres, to Kim Arrington, to Margaret Chapman, to Namia Coster, to Mitch Cox, to Justine LaMantia Daniel, to Tracie Fellers, to Mark Greenstreet to Ting Lam, to Julie Lemanski, to Alec Lowman, to Ormand Moore, to Scott Reintgen, to Cassie Rooney, Leslie Schwartz, to Crystal Simone Smith, to Dan Wales, to Meg Williamson, to Brooke Willis, to John Wood, to Barry Yeoman, to Gideon Young. And to Thomas Patterson for the space to make writing happen. And to all of our students of the past, of the present, and in the future.

Gratitude for family. To all eight of my brothers and sisters: Donald Ray, Karen, Sylvester, Sylvia, John, Ruby, Gloria, Sherman, to all my nieces and nephews, to my father, Sylvester W. Dublin, to my mother, Geraldine Blackwell Dublin, to my grandmothers, to the grandfather who I was able to meet and to the one who passed before I came to be, to all of our ancestors and their kin. I will try to live a life worthy of your sacrifices. I will try to teach my own children to live even more worthy lives than me, to my children, Darien and River.

To everyone else who is a part of this collection in one part or another. To Rebecca Berkley, to Chary Gumeta, Isai Lara, to Amy Nelder, to Christopher Pendergraft, to Kanetha Azar Ramsey, to May Star, to Ingrid Valencia, to Jantzen Zink, to the softest skin in Golden Hill, to the woman I met once who gave me a name in sign language. Thank you to all others who remain nameless but retain a place in my heart. Light to anyone I have temporarily forgotten.

And the most special thank you to Mary Katherine Lewin, puzzle piece with whom I fit.

VIDEO POEMS

Video poetry (also known as videopoetry, film poetry, video-visual poetry, or cinépoetry) is the narrative, non-narrative, or anti-narrative combination of poetry and video/film in the form of text, sound, and image that results in what Tom Konyves, an early video poetry artist, calls "a poetic experience." What you can access below is a playlist of video poems created by Kevin Dublin for *How to Fall in Love in San Diego*.

https://bit.ly/HTFIL-VIDEOS

About the Author

Kevin Dublin is an educator, filmmaker, economic justice advocate, and a writer of poetry, prose, scripts, and code. He is the recipient of fellowships and awards from the San Francisco Arts Commission, Center for Cultural Innovation, Martha's Vineyard Institute of Creative Writing, and more. His work has appeared in *Ploughshares*, *Konch*, *Apocrypha Magazine*, *The San Franciscan*, *North Carolina Literary Review*, *Cincinnati Review*, and several international poetry anthologies. Kevin is the founder of The Living Room SF and is also the author of *Eulogy* (Raven & Wren Press, 2023). He resides in San Francisco, holds a BFA in Creative Writing & BA in Writing & Technology from the University of North Carolina at Wilmington, MA in English from East Carolina University, as well as an MFA in Poetry from San Diego State, and for a little Black boy from Smithfield, NC, believes he has been brought a mighty long way.

www.ingramcontent.com/pod-product-compliance
Lightning Source LLC
Chambersburg PA
CBHW060542080526
44586CB00012B/825